Zebra's Tent

Written and illustrated by
Laura Hambleton

Collins

Sheep got snacks from his bright red backpack.

"Yum, sweets!" said Croc.

4

Zebra got cups for the drink and Duck got spoons for the yogurt.

"Look at my pink and green dressing up box," said Zebra.

Croc took the bright green hat.
"I'm looking good!" he boasted.

Sheep sang a sweet song and Duck had a bang on the drum.

Zebra said, "We must sleep soon.
It is dark."

"I will sweep up the mess," said Sheep,
getting a broom.

Duck collected the green sheets
and Croc got the books.

"Is it a thunderstorm?" said Croc in fright.
"Or a spook?" said Sheep, feeling afraid.

"It is not a spook! It is my mum!" said Zebra.

Mum had mugs and brown toast.

Zebra's tent

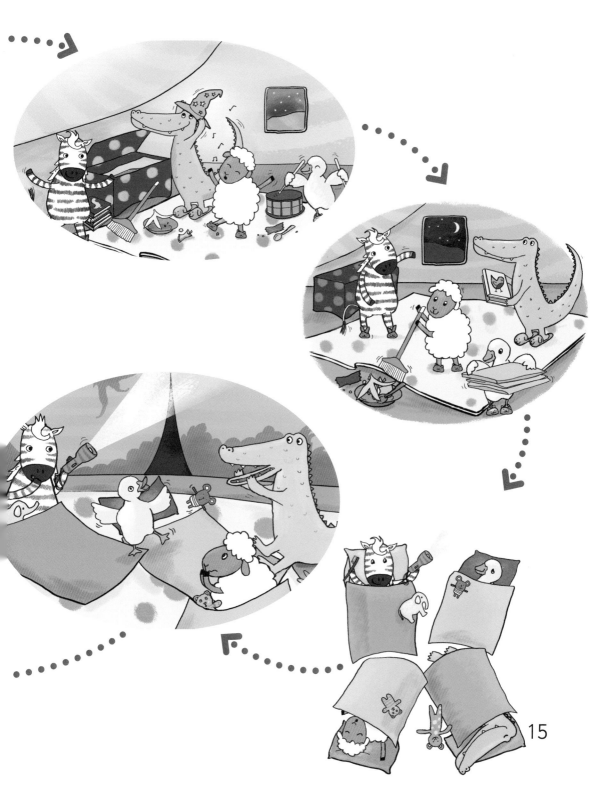

Review: After reading

Use your assessment from hearing the children read to choose any GPCs, words or tricky words that need additional practice.

Read 1: Decoding
- Look through the book together to find words that begin with adjacent consonants (e.g. **stars**, **br**ight).
- Repeat to find words that end with adjacent consonants (e.g. *tent*, *pink*).
- Take turns with the children to point to and read words from the book that contain two syllables. (e.g. *back/pack*, *yo/gurt*)

Read 2: Prosody
- Model reading each page with expression to the children.
- After you have read each page, ask the children to have a go at reading with expression.
- Read the book together using different voices for the animals.
- On pages 10 and 11, take turns to read the main text and noises. For page 11, encourage the children to use expression to show how the animals are feeling.

Read 3: Comprehension
- Turn to pages 14 and 15 and ask the children to retell the story in their own words, using the pictures as prompts.
- For every question ask the children how they know the answer. Ask:
    - What snacks do the animals eat in the tent? (e.g. *sweets*, *yogurt*)
    - Are the animals excited or scared when they hear noises outside? (e.g. *They are scared because they shot up in fright.*)
    - How do you think the animals are feeling by the end of the story? (e.g. *They are happy and sleepy because Mum came and it is time for bed.*)
    - Do you still feel the same about staying in Zebra's tent as you did before we read the book? Explain why.